THE JEWISH QUARTERLY

The Jewish Quarterly is published four times a year
by The Jewish Quarterly Pty Ltd

Publisher: Morry Schwartz

ISBN 9781760645342 E-ISBN 9781743823774
ISSN 0449010X E-ISSN 23262516

ALL RIGHTS RESERVED.
No part of this publication may be reproduced, stored in a retrieval system
or transmitted in any form by any means electronic, mechanical, photocopying,
recording or otherwise without the prior consent of the publishers.

Essay © retained by the author

Subscriptions 1 year print & digital (4 issues): $74.99 AUD | £42 GBP | $56 USD.
1 year digital only: $44.99 AUD | £25 GBP | $32 USD. Payment may be made by
Mastercard or Visa. Payment includes postage and handling.

Subscribe online at jewishquarterly.com or email subscribe@jewishquarterly.com
Email enquiries@jewishquarterly.com

The Jewish Quarterly is published under licence from the
Jewish Literary Trust Limited, which exercises a governance function.

UK Company Number: 01189861. UK Charity Commission Number: 268589.

Directors of the Jewish Literary Trust: Michael Mocatta (co-chair),
Andrew Renton (co-chair), Lance Blackstone (chair emeritus), Devorah Baum,
Phillip Blumberg, Ian Buruma, John Cohen, Shelly Freeman, Larraine Solomons,
Michael Strelitz.

Founding Editor: Jacob Sonntag

Editor: Jonathan Pearlman.

Issue 256, May 2024

THE JEWISH QUARTERLY

Blindness

October 7 and the left

Hadley Freeman is a journalist and author. Her books include *House of Glass: The Story and Secrets of a Twentieth-Century Jewish Family* and *Good Girls: A Story and Study of Anorexia*.

Blindness

October 7 and the left

Hadley Freeman

October 8

October 7 was horrific. Hamas terrorists stormed into southern Israel to rape, kidnap and kill Jews. They fulfilled their mission. Parents were tortured in front of their children, children were butchered in front of their parents. Young people were chased down and slaughtered at a music festival. People burned alive. Babies mutilated. And all the while, Hamas fighters cheered and jeered on social media and in the GoPro footage they recorded. Twelve hundred people were killed. Two hundred and fifty people were kidnapped.

Then came October 8, and that's when Jews understood how hated they really are.

In cities around the world, including Brighton and New York City – bastions of liberal sensibility, homes to thousands of Jews – protests were held. But not against Hamas, who were at that moment still wiping the blood of Israelis off their boots. Against Israel. On October 9 – before Israel had even started to retaliate – protestors in Sydney waved Palestinian flags and chanted "Fuck the Jews" while burning an Israeli flag. There were protests outside the Israeli embassy in London; my parents could see the flares and hear the chants from their apartment. On October 7 itself, thirty-four Harvard student organisations issued a statement that they "hold the Israeli regime entirely responsible for all the unfolding violence". This is the generation raised on the beliefs that "victim blaming" is wrong and "microaggressions" – which Harvard has defined as "verbal or nonverbal slights/insults (whether intentional or unintentional) that negatively targeted a particular identity group" – are unacceptable. But I guess massacring Jews is too micro to count.

More and more footage from October 7 kept being released: terrified young women with the crotches of their trousers stained with blood; elderly Holocaust survivors carted off on trucks; children dragged away from their homes. There were reports of whole families tortured and murdered at their breakfast tables. There was audio of the terrorists cheering about "killing Jews". And still, the reactions from protesters in the street ranged from silent to sceptical to celebratory. At the time, this seemed inexplicable. But it soon became predictable. Over the next few months, anti-Israel protests happened so regularly in London that I stopped taking my children into town on the weekends, because they were bewildered by all the placards warning about "Zionist racism" and "Jewish apartheid" carried by people who looked like they could be our neighbours. Attendance at their Hebrew school plummeted, because, presumably, parents were scared someone might attack the building, or maybe they just didn't want to encounter the weekend protestors. One afternoon in November when I arrived at the school to pick them up, a bus was nearby with Palestinian flags draped in the window and the driver was honking his horn continually. "Fuck Jewish genocide!" a man on the bus shouted at my children and me as we crossed the road to get away.

> *"I thought Jews had a freehold in Britain. But it turns out we were just renting"*

Since October 7, Jews around the world have become accustomed to this kind of antisemitic rhetoric, which has the propulsive viciousness of a bullet that was just waiting for the right trigger to blow it out of the gun. It is no longer a surprise, but it is still shocking. "I thought Jews had a freehold in Britain. But it turns out we were just renting," my friend the journalist

Tanya Gold said to me one Saturday morning at our synagogue. The night of October 7, I posted links on my private social media – which only people I personally know can see – to stories that had some of the few, terrifying details that were known so far about the pogrom. I immediately got two direct messages: one from a French art gallery owner who lives in London, berating me for falling for Israeli propaganda; the other from a books editor, explaining that Israel is an apartheid state and including a link to the history of slave uprisings. I quietly unfollowed friends on Instagram as they posted videos of themselves chanting "From the river to the sea" at the marches in London and New York, with long, chin-stroking captions railing against Israel's bombing of Gaza, but never mentioning – not once – October 7, the hostages or even Hamas.

By now, several months into the conflict, with Gaza destroyed, thousands and thousands of Palestinian children orphaned and killed, and the Palestinians in desperate need of food and aid, I know some people will say that to focus on October 7 is wrong. That it reveals a skewing of priorities, a perverse narcissism, a fetishisation of Jewish victimhood. Israel is fine. It's the Palestinians we should be worrying about now, okay?

Of course we should worry about the Palestinians. Jews know this better than most. The vast majority of the Diaspora has long been highly critical of the settlements in the West Bank, the occupation and, most of all, the religious fundamentalism that is now inextricable from Israel's far right. Most Jews around the world feel a strong connection with Israel, but they very much do not feel one with Netanyahu and his far-right government, and many have spoken out over the years about their cruelty towards the Palestinians. The Palestinian leadership has also failed its people too, miserably and repeatedly, and none more so than Hamas, which has about as much interest in the welfare of the Palestinians as it has in that of Israelis. And we now know exactly how demonic Hamas are because they filmed what they did to the Israelis on October 7 and uploaded it to social media so we could see it.

We know, thanks to the footage and the accounts of first responders, that an Israeli woman had nails in her vagina; another had her breasts sliced off. We know Israeli men and women were sexually assaulted and then shot in their genitals. Everyone is horrified by what is happening to the Palestinians; what is striking is that so many have withheld similar concern for the Israelis. Even after Israel collected the evidence from Hamas's own cameras and showed it around the world in a film titled *Bearing Witness*, many people on social media, including some with high profiles, dismissed it as "PR" and not evidence of rape, despite the images of dead women naked below the waist. It's enough to almost make you feel sorry for Hamas: they filmed what they did and made it available and *still* some people refuse to believe it. What's a terrorist gotta do to get some credit around here?

People have a strange reluctance to see Jews as victims, even when the facts are right there. When Bergen-Belsen was liberated in 1945, journalist Richard Dimbleby reported from the camp what he saw – yet the BBC didn't want to broadcast the report. Eventually they allowed it, but only after his script was cut in half. His son Jonathan later said that "the BBC needed more sources to support what had happened to Jews and worried that if you mentioned one group of people and not others, it might seem biased or wrong".

Minimising and even denying the extent of the carnage on October 7 is the new form of Holocaust denial, a specific kind of trauma inflicted specifically and sadistically on Jews. What other country would be attacked and then be derided and vilified? What other minority would need to provide video footage of what terrorists did to them, and still not be believed?

Most people, I once believed, are capable of feeling compassion for the Palestinians, and also horror at what happened on October 7. But since October 8, I don't believe that anymore. Too many have convinced themselves that all Israelis – all Jews – are bad in order to defend the Palestinians, whom they need to see as pure, oppressed victims. And so facts are twisted, truths conveniently ignored. The people who write "CEASEFIRE NOW" all over their social media are either ignorant of or uninterested in the fact that there had been a ceasefire between Hamas and Israel, until Hamas broke it. ("There's an ellipsis at the end of that demand," the solicitor and chair of law and the arts at University College London Anthony Julius said to me. "What those people are really saying is, 'Ceasefire now ... while Hamas re-arm.'") They don't care that Hamas will never honour a ceasefire, and they don't care that Hamas hates women and gay people, never mind Jews. They don't care that hundreds of thousands of Israelis had been protesting against Netanyahu for much of the past year, and so were hardly in lockstep with him, and no one cares that these allegedly pro-Palestinian supporters around the world were protesting against Israel before –

> *University campuses have been the sites of some of the most shocking examples of antisemitic incidents*

this cannot be repeated enough – before Israel had even retaliated. It was as if, the day after 9/11, people I thought of as friends had cheered for Osama bin Laden.

In the weeks after October 7, antisemitic hate crimes in London – such as attacks on Jewish schools and shops – exploded by 1350 per cent compared with the same period the year before; Islamophobic hate crimes also increased by 140 per cent in that time – an appalling increase, but a tenth of what Jews were experiencing. In the United States, anti-Jewish attacks increased by 400 per cent; in Germany, 240 per cent; in France, almost 100 per cent.

University campuses have been the sites of some of the most shocking, and the most visible, examples of antisemitic incidents since October 7. On American campuses, from autumn 2022 to autumn 2023 there was an increase of 700 per cent – "and last autumn was already our all-time high of reported antisemitic incidents", Jonathan Falk, the vice-president of Israel Action and Addressing Anti-Semitism Program for Hillel International, the largest Jewish campus organisation in the world, told me.

> So now it's seven times that. And it's not just the increase but the directness and the severity of the attacks that scare me. It's one thing to see a swastika on a bathroom stall door. But now we're getting reports like a student coming back to their dorm after the break and someone stole their mezuzah and wrote "Free Palestine" on their door. That kind of directness is scary.

From October to December 2023, Hillel International recorded 683 antisemitic incidents on 132 North American campuses, ranging from vandalism to hate speech to physical assault.

There were thirty-nine physical assaults of Jewish students from those campuses in those three months. That is more than in the entire previous decade. In late October at the Cooper Union college in New York City, Jewish students were trapped in a locked library while other students banged on the windows and doors chanting "Free Palestine". At the University of Massachusetts Amherst in early November, a Jewish student was punched in the face when he said he was attending a vigil for the Israeli hostages. At Berkeley, Jewish students were forced to hide in basements and tunnels while their fellow students banged on the doors and windows outside, shouting about genocide.

That same weekend, I happened to be visiting Harvard and multiple Jewish students there told me that their fellow students – "white kids who couldn't identify Gaza on a map", as one put it – had targeted them and accused them of genocide, not because they want to kill Palestinians, which they very much don't, but because they believe in Israel's right to exist. "And there's no point in complaining about this to the administration, because they either agree with that, or they're too scared to say anything," another Jewish student told me. (Almost all the Jewish students I spoke to asked not to be identified out of fear they'd be further targeted.)

In December, the presidents of Harvard, Massachusetts Institute of Technology and the University of Pennsylvania testified at a congressional hearing about antisemitism on college campuses. In a much-watched exchange, they were questioned by Republican congresswoman Elise Stefanik about, among other things, why Harvard allowed a Ukrainian flag to fly on campus but not an Israeli one; why the notoriously antisemitic Pink Floyd bassist Roger Waters was invited to speak at a Penn literary festival; and why students on the campuses were allowed to chant in support for a global intifada. Stefanik asked if calling for "the genocide of Jews" – her widely shared interpretation of the call for intifada – was against the rules on their campuses. "It depends on the context," they replied.

Shortly after their testimonies, Penn president Elizabeth Magill resigned. Claudine Gay, president of Harvard, resigned the following month in the wake of accusations of plagiarism. But the world had seen how life had deteriorated for Jewish students on campuses. "We have to remember that students look to the president of a university, and if they can't say, 'Antisemitism is wrong, it cannot be allowed,' we'll see more hate," says Falk.

Many people on the left – as well as Gay herself – complained afterwards that the hearing had been "a well-laid trap" (one which Gay was very well paid to avoid, and failed). Moreover, because Stefanik is a Trump-supporting Republican, she was accused of "weaponising antisemitism" against America's liberal higher education institutions. This is a standard tactic adopted by people who can't deny the message, and so complain about the messenger. After all, you can't "weaponise" antisemitism – a tedious zeitgeist term for "exploiting" antisemitism – if antisemitism isn't there to be weaponised.

"No doubt right-wing people weaponise antisemitism, as the Tories did during the Corbyn years in the UK. But that did not mean Labour *wasn't* antisemitic, and it was the same story with the congressional hearings," says the writer David Baddiel.

> But when people say things like, "Oh, this was just weaponising antisemitism," I say, "Try to think of Jews as real human beings." So when Elise Stefanik is weaponising antisemitism for her own Republican reasons, don't think about her. Think about Jews listening to that video. Think about them listening to these people who are not prepared to condemn the genocide of Jews. Those are the people who matter in that conversation.

Jewish parents and students definitely heard it. "We are now hearing from parents asking if there will be armed security at Hillel Shabbat dinners and other Jewish events on campuses," says Falk. "That is something we have never heard before. And we're adding cameras and taking security measures that are totally new."

This wasn't limited to American college campuses. At Birmingham University in the UK, there was a march in February in which activists allegedly chanted "Death to Zionists!" and held up a banner proclaiming "Zionists off our campus!" That same month, "Free Palestine" was sprayed in graffiti on the campus's Hillel House, and the Leeds University chaplain Rabbi Zaccharia Deutsch had to go into hiding after returning from Israel, where he'd been serving with his reserve unit. The Muslim Association of Britain posted a statement aimed at Leeds University, saying, "How can your students feel safe with a war criminal complicit in genocide roaming your campus?"

In November 2023, Anthony Julius wrote in *The Sunday Times* about the local branch of the lecturers' union at his university passing a motion calling for "intifada until victory" – a phrase that goes far beyond a plea for Palestinian statehood, and is instead an explicit threat against Israel and the Diaspora. "The university's Jewish studies department notifies students of lecture venues by text, for fear of disruption," he wrote. "Students at Jewish Society lunches are protected by security guards. Jewish students stay on campus for only as long as they need to, and then leave. The general sentiment is, better to conceal all signs of their Jewishness."

In January 2024, I asked Julius how the university had responded to his article. "That's what really shocked me," he replied. "I know the provost of my university read it, as did all the senior faculty, and not one of them spoke to me about it. None. Because they don't care. If I was an academic from another minority community and I wrote about prejudice at UCL in such trenchant terms, do you think for one second that the university would ignore it? It seems unlikely."

Is it because they think Jews are privileged, so it doesn't matter?

"I think it's an older trope than that: they think Jews are liars. After all, if there's an allegation of racism, an institution like UCL would take it very seriously. But if there's one of antisemitism, the reaction is, 'Let's appoint someone to see whether it's really antisemitism or if the Jews are lying again.'" A Jewish student at a UK university put it to me like this: "When a student from a minority background complains about bigotry, we all need to do the work. When I complain about antisemitism, it's another Jew trying to control things again."

> *This – undeniably, overwhelmingly – feels different for all Jews*

It is true that some Jews say that every criticism of Israel is antisemitic and claim to hear bigotry in the most innocuous statement – like Alvy Singer (Woody Allen) in *Annie Hall* insisting that even a question about lunch was insulting. ("He didn't say, 'Did you eat?' He said, 'Jew, eat.' Jew!") But the inverse is rarely noted: in my experience, more Jews commit an enormous amount of emotional labour trying to convince themselves that the abuse they're hearing is really just hatred of Israel rather than hatred of Jews. Because who wants to believe the latter?

But after October 7, even the most fervent denialists among us saw it. Many Jews I know stopped wearing their yarmulkes outside in case it made them a target. "This feels different," is what we all keep saying. This feels different from all the previous international reactions to wars in the Middle East; this feels different to other brushes with antisemitism we've seen in the West in recent years, from the Jeremy Corbyn scandal in the UK to the murders in the Tree of Life Synagogue in Pittsburgh in 2018; this feels different to all the previous backlashes against Benjamin Netanyahu and his government. This – undeniably, overwhelmingly – feels different for all Jews.

Something has broken, or maybe it has become unmoored. When I was a teenager in the 1990s, it seemed to me there was a collective understanding that the Holocaust had been the bonfire that showed the worst of humanity and therefore antisemitism was not a match to be trifled with. Every writer I read – Martin Amis, Philip Roth, Sylvia Plath – reinforced this; every politician I saw on TV repeated it. But somewhere, in the past three decades, that understanding has dimmed. Holocaust Memorial Day (HMD, known outside Britain as Holocaust Remembrance Day) falls every year on January 27, the anniversary of when

Auschwitz-Birkenau was liberated by the Soviets. And yet HMD is no longer about the 6 million Jews killed in the Holocaust but "all victims of genocide", and any Jew foolish enough to query this shift is firmly reprimanded for being exclusionary. (That was the real problem with the Holocaust: not inclusive enough.)

At the end of 2023, a historian friend of mine, who was writing a book about the concentration camps, was told solemnly by her editor that she had to make clear the Holocaust wasn't *just* about the Jews: it was also about gay people, Romani, trans people. "The Nazis hated lots of people. But the Holocaust was specifically a genocide of the Jews," my friend replied, anxious not to annoy her editor. "It was about a lot of people," the editor said irritably, condescendingly and wrongly. The industrial annihilation of two-thirds of Europe's Jews is now just another blip in the annals of history, nothing extraordinary. And in fact, maybe it wasn't about the Jews at all: increasingly they're not even mentioned on Holocaust Memorial Day for – waves hands vaguely around – *reasons*. On January 27, 2024, the first HMD after October 7, the secretary-general of the UN and the Scottish first minister omitted any reference to the Jews at all when marking the day. They succeeded where Hitler failed and erased Jews from their own history. Historical memory that had once been so vivid is fading and, with it, a truth that had been understood and agreed upon is slipping away.

"Criticise the Israeli government, by all means," we liberal Jews have been saying for decades, keen to prove our lack of bias. But it turns out that what people seemed to hear was: "Hate Israel and all who live in it."

"For a lot of Jews, in New York and in other cities, the past few months have been a real shock. It was very, very painful to see the indifference people had to October 7," Justin Finkelstein, an analyst with the Anti-Defamation League's Center on Extremism in New York City, tells me. "A lot of Jews in New York identify more on the left side of the political spectrum and they feel anywhere from ignored to betrayed by folks who call themselves progressives."

Antisemitism has always been an equal-opportunity hatred, one enjoyed by both the right and the left. Like misogyny, for that matter. Not very long ago, there was a neat schism in the stereotyping: to the far right, Jews were swarthy communists and Bolsheviks plotting to destabilise – and contaminate – the West. Meanwhile, the far left portrayed them as ultra-white, ultra-wealthy capitalists propping up an unfair system for their own benefit. In recent years, there has been a flattening of the tropes: both sides generally portray Jews as rich, powerful and extremely clannish. Proof, I guess, that even in today's extremely partisan politics, the right and left can come together on one issue.

When Jews talk about modern left-wing antisemitism, the most common response from the left is that they're not antisemitic, they're anti-Zionist, and even if some of them are antisemitic, it's not important because the antisemitism from the far right is far more dangerous. Well, rest assured, goysplainers, we know how bad antisemitism is from fascists. Many of us have lost large branches of our family tree to it. As recently as 2017 we watched men carrying tiki torches through Charlottesville, Virginia, chanting "Jews will not replace us", and we heard the then US president, Donald Trump, describe them as "very fine people". So maybe it's because we focused so much on antisemitism from the right that we missed what was happening at the other end of the ideological spectrum. Because what shocked so many of us after October 7 was the hate from the left.

> *To the progressive left, there is a progressive way to see the world and a wrong way to see the world*

"The left" is a big term. The specific faction of the left that I mean, the one that reacted most virulently against Israel, is variously known as the progressive left, the identarian left, the online left, the intersectional left or the woke left. It is the left that is so popular on college campuses, among the faculty and students. The centre left, or liberal left, celebrates pluralism and pragmatism. The progressive left regards such values as self-deluding weaknesses. To the progressive left, there is a progressive way to see the world and a wrong way to see the world, and anyone who sees it wrongly is akin to a fascist. A few decades ago it was known as the far left or hard left, when its focus was class oppression. Now it is identity oppression. Yet as Baddiel famously pointed out in his bestselling 2021 book about antisemitism, *Jews Don't Count*, when it comes to identity politics and an awareness of vulnerable minority groups, to the far left, Jews really don't count.

The October 8 protest in New York City was promoted by the Democratic Socialists of America, flagbearers for America's progressive left. When some raised objections to it – including the DSA's most prominent figurehead, Representative Alexandria Ocasio-Cortez – the DSA conceded there had been "confusion". But, they added, "we are also concerned that some have chosen to focus on a rally while ignoring the root causes of violence in the region, the far-right Netanyahu government's escalating human rights violations and explicitly genocidal rhetoric, and the dehumanization of the Palestinian people." (If the DSA think the "root cause" of violence in the Middle East is Netanyahu, have I got an Old Testament to show them …) Rivkah Brown, an editor at the far-left UK publication *Novara*, tweeted on the day that October 7 "should be a day of celebration for supporters of democracy and human rights worldwide". On October 10, the Chicago chapter of Black Lives Matter tweeted an image of a paraglider with a Palestinian flag, appearing to celebrate the terrorists who slaughtered 250 people at Nova, the Israeli dance music festival.

Both Brown and BLM Chicago later apologised and deleted their posts, but throughout the rest of October, open letters were signed by good leftie celebrities such as Tilda Swinton and Steve Coogan and published in publications like the *London Review of Books*, *ArtForum* and even *Vogue*. They all condemned Israel; they didn't mention October 7, the hostages or Hamas. All of the blame for Palestinian suffering was being directed at Israel and none at Hamas, which allegedly had been planning October 7 for years, but spent none of that time preparing for the safety of its citizens during Israel's entirely foreseeable response. This is in keeping with Hamas's longstanding practice of using Palestinians as human shields, spending all their money on tunnels and weaponry and none on their citizens. But acknowledging these practices complicates the progressive left's binary view of Israel as the genocidal oppressor and anyone on the other side as the pure victim. Even when the other side's founding charter explicitly calls for the genocide of Jews, as Hamas's does.

"The terror attack on Israel by Hamas has been a divisive – if clarifying – moment for the left," the journalist Helen Lewis wrote. "The test that it presented was simple: ... Can you lay down, for a moment, your legitimate criticisms of Benjamin

Netanyahu's government ... and express horror at the mass murder of civilians?" For many, the answer was equally simple: no.

"I think you can divide it in two," Alex Hearn, co-director of Labour Against Anti-Semitism, told me. "There are some on the left who reacted very empathetically to October 7, and they can see that some of the wider fallout from it is part of a bigger, dangerous pattern and are horrified by it. As you'd expect. And then there is the far left, who think of themselves as good people, and since October 7 they've become more antisemitic than ever."

When Russia invaded Ukraine, many of my neighbours in my very liberal area of North London put Ukrainian flags in their windows and have kept them there since. All the local schools held talks for their students about racism during the rise of the Black Lives Matter movement, especially after the murder of George Floyd thousands of miles away. And yet, after innocent Israelis were attacked, raped and murdered, there were and are no Israeli flags in anyone's window near me, and not one school that I know of held any talks about the atrocity. On October 9, I went to a vigil for Israel opposite Downing Street, organised by the Board of Deputies of British Jews, the largest communal Jewish organisation in Britain. It was widely publicised across social media and Israel hadn't yet started its determined retaliation. But when I got there, I was struck by how small the gathering was, certainly smaller than the pro-Palestinian protests erupting around the world. Most of the men I saw were wearing kippahs and tallits. Everyone around me knew the Hebrew prayers and the *Hatikvah*. Everyone, in other words, seemed to be Jewish. Why were only Jews showing solidarity with Israel and the victims of the Hamas pogrom?

Showing sympathy for Israel was, I kept being told, "complicated". October 7 "did not happen in a vacuum", as UN secretary-general António Guterres put it in late October. There was "context". And it's true, there is a context. There is always context. But "context" in this circumstance felt increasingly like a euphemism for "this was justified". "It's not wrong to say everything should be seen in context," says Baddiel. "But the call here for contextualisation tended to come with something it doesn't come with when talking about other atrocities, which is that we shouldn't consider this an atrocity. We should lessen our outrage about it. And that was striking."

> *As sympathetic as I am to the Palestinian cause, I didn't feel like these were marches I could attend*

This nervy silence – or worse – from people the Jewish left had considered natural allies has pushed many of us into unfamiliar spaces. "I've spent my life being not that interested in the State of Israel," Baddiel says. He barely mentioned Israel in *Jews Don't Count* – partly because he felt no connection to "that foreign country", but also partly because he wanted to separate antisemitism, an ancient bigotry, from being anti-Israel or anti-Zionist, which he saw as a more geopolitical position. But when he heard progressives describing October 7 as "an act of resistance", he knew something was shifting: "The ANC [in South Africa] and the IRA [in Northern Ireland] did not glory in the dehumanisation of their victims, the way Hamas did," he explains.

> The ANC and the IRA used violent means for political ends, and while there may have been elements of that here, it was the triumphal despoiling of the victims and the references to "killing Jews" that felt undeniably antisemitic to me. But because certain parts of the progressive left don't want to see Jews as victims, you get this denialism, and then I think, "Oh fuck, I'm now in a conversation about Israel."

I have never avoided talking about Israel. Ever since I was old enough to understand the history of Israel, I have supported a two-state solution. Like any sentient person, I loathe the oppressive regime in the West Bank and Netanyahu's anti-Palestinian policies. After October 7, I felt enormous sympathy for the

Palestinians, whom I knew would be bombed to kingdom come by Israel as it destroyed Gaza in its determination to destroy Hamas.

I understood why some people felt showing sympathy to Israel might be complicated, if they saw October 7 as the latest episode in a long and bloody battle. But why was that same standard not applied to the Palestinians? Did October 7 not count as "context"? Apparently not. My social media feed was soon filled with images and videos of the weekly pro-Palestine marches, posted by people I consider friends, carrying signs referring to Israelis as "colonisers" and chanting "From the river to the sea". But as sympathetic as I am to the Palestinian cause, I didn't feel like these were marches I could attend. They felt like marches not so much in favour of Palestinian rights and statehood, but against anyone who believes Israel has a right to exist. "From the river to the sea" means that all the land between the River Jordan and the Mediterranean Sea should be Palestinian – that is, that Israel shouldn't exist at all. Was this the pro-Palestinian position now?

"I believe there should be a Palestinian state and I have worked towards the creation of a Palestinian state for many years, one that is distinct in name and will bring real equality and justice," says Atira Winchester, the director of content and leadership at the New Israel Fund, a progressive non-profit aimed at bringing social justice and equality to Israelis and Palestinians in Israeli territories.

And yet there is no part of me that feels I can go on the pro-Palestinian marches. There are a lot of people on those marches who have a very aggressive agenda, but that could have been counteracted by the leadership, who could have actively reached out and made space for people from other communities, and that has not happened at all. I understand it, but I also think it's deeply tragic.

As I mentioned, my parents live near the Israeli embassy in London, and so every weekend since October 7, loud demonstrations have swamped their neighbourhood. I take my kids to see their grandparents most weekends – now taking a circuitous route from the north to avoid the worst of the protests. The marches are a fascinatingly unlikely melange of different interest groups. There are the activist Muslim groups, some of whom travel in from outside of London – I see the coaches, draped in Palestine flags, going past my home in North London – and some of whom hold outright antisemitic and virulently anti-Israel placards. There are the older socialist-worker types, holding posters talking about Zionist capitalism and money. And finally the younger progressives, with posters comparing Netanyahu to Hitler. A toxic soup, all united now by one purpose: a hatred of Zionists.

Whenever a member of the public or a right-wing columnist suggests that a politician isn't *really* British or American because he or she is the child of immigrants – London mayor Sadiq Khan, say, or US vice-president Kamala Harris – people on the left react with horror. How dare you suggest that someone isn't truly of the country where they were born and raised? And yet those same people, who proudly describe themselves as "anti-racist" in their social media bios, now appear to be arguing that Jewish Israeli families – many of whom have lived in the country for over seventy-five years – have no right to be there and, by extension, brought their mutilations and murders on themselves. As a position for so-called leftists, it is astonishing.

One of the absolute shibboleths of the left is that a country should welcome refugees. And

> *Almost every Jew in Israel is descended from someone who needed to escape persecution*

yet not, it seems, when it comes to Jews migrating to Israel. I look at the people on the marches, people who surely bemoan the Republicans' and Tories' cruelty to immigrants, and I hear them describing Israelis as "colonialists" and "settlers". Do they not know *why* the Jews had to settle in Israel, or do they just not care? Did they really miss the Holocaust lessons in school? The few members of my Polish family who survived the camps couldn't go back to their native country because there were still pogroms there, such as the Kielce pogrom of 1946. And so they went to Israel, where Jewish roots date back millennia. Can refugees be called colonisers? Almost every Jew in Israel is descended from someone who needed to escape persecution – whether in Europe or other countries in the Middle East. And now their grandchildren and great-grandchildren are being killed for it, and the progressive left is defending this.

Jews have been told they don't belong in the places they live for as long as the Bible and history have recorded. That they are not true citizens; they are rootless, wandering Jews. The founding of Israel was intended as a corrective to that: no one could say Jews didn't belong in the Jewish homeland, right? As Jews learned on October 7, they absolutely could.

Examples of progressive anti-Israel politics heavily shading into antisemitism quickly became so numerous it's impossible to pick out the most egregious. Perhaps the most bleakly amusing was in December 2023, when a lesbian couple in Queensland changed their mind about using the sperm of a Jewish donor because, they explained in a message he posted on social media, they "don't have the capacity to navigate parts of your identity in this donor relationship". Fair enough. Everyone knows that babies with Jewish DNA instinctively start destroying Gaza before even teething, and that is a very tricky stage for a couple to navigate. Perhaps the most flat-out deluded was in January 2024, when pro-Palestine protestors shouted jeers outside the Memorial

Sloan Kettering Cancer Center – which also has a paediatric day hospital – in New York City, because Sloan Kettering had accepted a large financial donation from Ken Griffin, a Jewish American Zionist. "Shame, you support genocide!" the protestors shouted at the hospital, while sick children and adults were visible through the windows. And then they rampaged through Manhattan, protesting outside Starbucks, Zara and other outlets they believed were somehow connected to Israel. When Russia, or India, or China committed atrocities, no one – as far as I know – called those countries illegitimate or protested outside companies owned by those countries. The Russian Orthodox synagogue near my parents' home in London did not have to call in extra security after Russia invaded Ukraine, but the synagogues where I had my Bat Mitzvah and where my children now go to Hebrew school have done so now. This only happened to Israel and Jews.

"Is this the 1920s? Are we leading up to something big?" Jews started to ask among themselves. Stories of our grandparents' lives in the last century – in Krakow, in Vienna, in Berlin, in Paris – were starting to bite. In my quiet enclave of North London, such fears felt self-indulgent. Then, one night in November, as I was walking home from the Tube, I spotted a woman I'd seen in the neighbourhood before, stomping down the road ahead of me with her dog. When I checked my phone before going to bed,

I saw that one of my neighbours, a Jewish journalist named Ami Kaufman, had posted a video of her from that very night. He had confronted her on the bridge in our neighbourhood because she was tearing down posters of the kidnapped Israelis. When Ami asked her why, she replied, "I am cleaning this shit off the streets." When Ami asked her why again, she pointed her finger in his face, asking, "Are you Zionist? Are you Zionist? Are you pro-genocide? Are you killing all the children?" "These are innocent people," Ami called after her as she walked off. "No, they're not!" she screamed back. And that was when I had spotted her, stomping away.

Of course I had noticed that someone was tearing down the hostage posters on the bridge. Every morning someone put them up, and every night someone tore them down, scattering the scraps of paper on the road like ashes. Putting up and tearing down posters had become one of the most visible forms of protest, on both sides, in the first few weeks after October 7. Snickering students in American universities were filmed tearing down posters of Israeli hostages in their dorm hallways, and teenagers and twenty-somethings were filmed doing the same in Central London. So when I saw the pieces of the hostage posters on the road – and one in the nearby bus shelter of a baby with "terrorist" scrawled over his face – I assumed it was being done by mischievous young people.

It wasn't. The *Daily Mail* spotted Ami's video and quickly identified the woman as Anna Laurini, an artist whose work is shown in ritzy London galleries. She is also an antisemitic conspiracy theorist who has blamed Jews for everything from 9/11 to Covid. She lives in the square at the end of my road. The next day, one of my neighbours took the mezuzah off her door frame.

The bridge became even more of a poster battle ground, with more being put up in the morning, and more torn-up shreds on the ground overnight, than ever before. A second woman was photographed tearing down the hostage posters. She looked like she was in her thirties, wearing the uniform of a dental assistant. When I wrote a column about the bridge for the *Sunday Times*, where I'm a staff writer, I was barraged with tweets telling me the posters were "propaganda" and being used to justify Israel's actions against the Palestinians. But one person's propaganda is another person's explanation – after all, if Hamas hadn't kidnapped these people and killed over a thousand more, Israel wouldn't be bombing Gaza. Others dismissed the posters as a "provocation": "Why put up posters of people from thousands of miles away?" I was asked repeatedly. The obvious

> *The real question was: why would some people want us to forget them?*

answer was so that people don't forget about the kidnapped Israelis. The real question was: why would some people want us to forget them?

On October 7, I never could have imagined how weird things would get. But I began to get an idea on October 8, when I first saw the photos from the protest in Union Square, New York, a place I have been countless times, now filled with people carrying signs saying "Resistance is justified" and "Globalise the intifada". I realised two things at once. First, for a protest to happen on the 8th, it must have been organised on the 7th. So while Hamas militants were raping women and burning their bodies, people around the world decided to organise protests saying it was the women's fault for being Israeli. Second, the feeling I was experiencing was something I'd last felt a long time ago. Twenty-two years and almost one month ago, to be precise. It was the shock of being hated.

I was in New York City on 9/11, in a hotel about twenty blocks away from the Twin Towers. I don't remember much of the day itself, but I remember September 12, 2001, very well: I trudged uptown, through smog that was actually debris from the collapsed towers, while people ran frantically through the streets carrying giant bottles of water they had just bought in case the expected apocalypse materialised. I was walking to the apartment of parents of a friend of mine, Cat Macrae, who was missing, and later confirmed to be dead, killed at her desk at the age of twenty-three. I spent that week sitting in her grieving parents' apartment, traumatised. As I read the *New York Times* at the table where I used to have breakfast with Cat after sleepovers, I remember feeling ashamed of my ignorance: how had I not realised how loathed America was?

I grew up in New York, but have lived most of my life in London, and when I eventually was able to get back to the UK about a week later, I received nothing but sympathy – from my friends for me personally, and from politicians on TV for my hometown. Yes, there were some far-left voices suggesting America had brought this on itself – Seumas Milne in *The Guardian*, Mary Beard in the *London Review of Books* – but these were so niche as to be irrelevant. Of course many people outside America – hell, many people inside America – hated George W. Bush, and God knows many didn't like a lot of America's foreign policies. But people weren't jeering at Americans on TV, and newspaper columnists weren't posting long videos insisting that America was exaggerating what had actually happened. No one was deriding Americans for the sins of the American government. No one was saying the victims deserved it for living in New York, or that they were mere collateral for the greater good of the revolution. But all that and more happened to Jews after October 7. And that's what feels different this time. How did we not realise how hated we are?

Israel

Tony Benn, a totemic figure of twentieth-century British left politics, had a story he loved to tell. It was from his days serving in the RAF during World War II. On VE Day, the story goes, he arrived at the Sha'ar HaGolan kibbutz, by the Golan Heights, where he was told the Allies had won. Benn was a far-left Zionist and was overwhelmed with happiness by the combination of the war ending and being on a kibbutz, which he saw as the epitome of socialist ideals. For decades afterwards, he was one of Israel's loudest supporters in the UK.

Up to the middle of the last century, Zionism was the default left-wing position in the West. Labour Party conferences consistently passed pro-Zionist motions, championed by social democrats and socialists. Communist leaders – who were often Jewish – endorsed Zionism. The American labour movement, in particular the unions, were among Israel's most helpful supporters, even before the country was founded. During the 1920s and '30s, the unions donated millions of dollars to the Histadrut, Israel's national labour union. After 1948, American unions invested in the country's bond programme – over US$1 billion by 1994. "In many ways, you can argue that US unions helped construct the state of Israel," Jeff Schuhrke, a labour historian at Empire State University, told the *New York Times* in January 2024.

You can trace the progressive left's shifting relationship with Israel through the US unions: in 1982, the American Federation of Labor and Congress of Industrial Organizations (AFL-CIO) took out a full-page advert in the *New York Times* to declare its support for Israel in the Israel–Lebanon War. Since October 7, multiple unions have been riven with internal arguments about Israel. On October 15 several screenwriters, including Jerry Seinfeld, sent an open letter to the Writers Guild of America to ask why they hadn't issued a statement condemning the pogrom. The guild had previously made public statements of support for #MeToo and the Black Lives Matters movement, the screenwriters wrote, but said nothing "when terrorists invaded Israel to murder, rape and kidnap Jews". Meredith Stiehm, the president of the Writers Guild of America West, then explained the guild's silence in an email to its members: "Like the membership itself, the board's viewpoints are varied, and we found consensus out of reach. For these reasons, we have decided not to comment publicly."

> *You're either entirely on-side or you're on the bad side*

Some have asked why, say, Starbucks Workers United needed to say anything at all about the war. ("Oh, the head of the Amazon Labor Unit posted 'From the river to the sea' on his social media?

Wow, that's made me rethink everything!" Netanyahu probably never said.) But it reflects broader generational changes: first, the younger generation joining unions now expect them to be an expression of their politics, as much as their social media is. There is no sense of individual compromise for the greater professional whole, no understanding that even people on your own team may have slightly different politics. You're either entirely on-side or you're on the bad side, an absolutist viewpoint that is an essential part of progressive politics. It also reflects the fact that young people joining unions today do not associate Israel with the Oslo Accords, let alone the Holocaust. They associate it with Netanyahu.

An even clearer illustration of how the progressive left has turned against Israel can be seen through *The Guardian* newspaper, the UK's most left-leaning mainstream broadsheet and my former employer. Over a decade ago, when *The Guardian* premises were on Farringdon Road in East London, a small *Guardian* museum briefly opened opposite the office, known as The Newsroom. In this museum, there was a carefully preserved letter from almost a century ago, written by Chaim Weizmann, a key figure of early Zionism, to C.P. Scott, *The Guardian*'s legendary editor from 1871 to 1929 (at that time the *Manchester Guardian*). In the letter, Weizmann thanks Scott for his support for Israel and tells him that when the history of Jews is written, Scott will be singled out as an especial friend. This is a souvenir from the improbable but close friendship between the two men, who happened to meet at a tea party in Manchester in 1914. In November of that year, Scott wrote to Weizmann, "I was immensely interested in what you told me of your hopes and plans. There are so few people who have the courage of an ideal and at the same time the insight and energy which make it possible."

Scott introduced Weizmann, a Russian Jew, to members of the British establishment, including David Lloyd George when he was the chancellor of the Exchequer. And Scott himself was energetic for the Zionist cause, joining the British Palestine Committee, which argued for British sponsorship of Zionism. After Lloyd George became prime minister, he introduced the Balfour Declaration in November 1917, which promised British support for a Jewish homeland in Palestine.

Just over 100 years later, in May 2021, *The Guardian* celebrated its bicentenary by, among other things, listing its worst mistakes over the years. (This was 2021: self-flagellation was very big on the left.) Alongside the paper's original support for the US Confederacy and asbestos, it included – yes – Scott's endorsement of the Balfour Declaration. "Whatever else can be said, Israel today is not the country *The Guardian* foresaw or would have wanted," the article's author, Randeep Ramesh, wrote.

This is undoubtedly true, but that does not mean Israel should never have existed, let alone that *The Guardian* shouldn't have endorsed the Balfour Declaration. The current situation was not inevitable – and it will one day, most people desperately hope, change. Nonetheless, *The Guardian* has gone from supporting Israel as a means to protect Jews from a potential genocide against them (9 November 1917) to running articles with headlines like "Israel Must Stop Weaponising the Holocaust" (24 October 2023).

"The left would say they've been completely consistent," says Jonathan Freedland, a staff writer at *The Guardian*. "They would say, 'We supported Israel when it was a small, fledgling country, and we stopped supporting it in 1967 when it became an occupier on the West Bank.'" This has merit to it. But the merit stops at the point when someone argues that Israel (or even the Balfour Declaration) should never have existed at all, and this has become the dominant line from the left, especially since October 7 – see the placards saying "75 Years of Occupation" at pro-Palestine marches around the world.

"That has been a big change," Freedland tells me. "Objecting to the occupation of the West Bank has been a mainstream left-wing position for a while. But delegitimisation of the whole country, of Israel – that is new, at least in the mainstream left, and that really took off during this conflict." Dave Rich, left-wing antisemitism expert and head of policy at a charity that provides security and advice to the British Jewish community, agrees. "What's happened over the past few years is that we now have a left for whom every conflict is about race, rather than class," he explains.

> It's all about white supremacy, systemic racism, power networks. All global oppressions are connected, according to this viewpoint, so there has been a BLM-ing of anti-Zionism, which says the entire country has been a colonialised country since 1948 and no one is talking anymore about [problems dating from] 1967, because that's not exciting enough and doesn't promise a cleansing of the world and a new utopia.

The idea that Israel is an occupied, illegitimate country lies behind much of the left's reaction to October 7. This is how people who consider themselves to be on the side of the oppressed, the just and the good convince themselves they are on the right side of history when they minimise or even cheer the rape, kidnapping and murder of Israeli civilians by fascist terrorists. To the left now, Israel is on par with apartheid South Africa, India under colonial rule, the antebellum South.

According to one *Guardian* columnist, when Israel was founded in 1948, the rest of the world "brazenly shrugged off three-quarters of a million Palestinians being driven from their homes 76 years ago, accompanied by an estimated 15,000 suffering violent deaths". This, the columnist wrote, planted "the seeds of today's bitter harvest". Going by this thinking, October 7 was a natural response to the colonialist foundation of Israel in 1948. Resistance is justified, and all that. Yet the people who talk with such concern about the events of 1948 never mention the 900,000 Jews who were kicked out of surrounding Arab countries in retaliation. One could almost say they have been brazenly shrugged off by the left.

A total ignorance of history is an essential element of the progressive left's reaction to October 7. For a start, many insist that it's not Jews they hate, it's just Zionists, although it's unclear how they square that with the fact that the vast majority of Jews are Zionists, and almost half of all Jews in the world live in Israel. It's like saying you don't hate the English, just the ones who think England is a legitimate country. At its most basic, the word "Zionist" means someone who believes Israel has a right to exist as a Jewish homeland. That's it. So if you're not a Zionist, you don't believe in a legally founded country.

Complaining about "Zionists" is the euphemistic way of complaining about Jews, as Jeremy Corbyn, the former leader of Britain's Labour Party, amply demonstrated at a 2013 conference in London convened by the Palestinian Return Centre. On the subject of British Zionists, Corbyn said they "clearly have two problems. One is they don't want to study history, and secondly, having lived in this country for a very long time, probably all their lives, they don't understand English irony either … So I think they needed two lessons, which perhaps we can help them with." The trope of Jews as foreign interlopers who don't know the local customs, no matter how long they've lived in a country, is so well known it does not need restating. (The irony is, of course, that if British Jews do have one collective characteristic, it's their highly developed sense of irony, whereas Corbyn is infamously the most humourless man to have ever been born in Britain.)

> *After October 7, the use of "Zionist" as a barely coded word for "Jew" became even more obvious*

After October 7, the use of "Zionist" as a barely coded word for "Jew" became even more obvious, as "anti-Zionism" became as much of a plank of progressive-left identity as anti-capitalism once was for the hard left. And, of course, the two things are connected. Left-wingers who insist they're not antisemitic, just anti-Zionist, are – knowingly or most likely not – carrying on a tradition that began with 1960s Soviet antisemitic propaganda, which said that Zionists were sabotaging the great communist project. The Soviet "Plan for Basic Organisational and Propaganda Measures Connected with the Situation in the Middle East and the Intensifying Struggle with Zionism" developed the now common tropes of comparing Israel with the Nazis and accusing the country of committing genocide, just as the historically ignorant on the pro-Palestine marches do today. They claimed – in proud Soviet tradition – that Israel was antithetical to the glorious communist cause, saying in a televised press conference that "Zionists supply imperialism with cannon fodder in the struggle against the Arab people". As the author and journalist Danny Finkelstein wrote in *The Times* in February:

> The Soviets wanted to recruit Arab governments and the Arab street to their side in the Cold War struggle with America. And virulent opposition to Israel helped them to do that. Similar forces are at work on the modern left. The adoption of obsessive antisemitism and the entertainment of wild anti-Israel and anti-Jewish conspiracy theories partly derives from theories about capitalism, but partly from political convenience.

This old link-up between the hard left and Arab countries explains the weird pass progressives give Hamas, who are outright fascists, while focusing their loathing on Israel. It also explains their willingness to march alongside open antisemites. Sure, their posters feature images of paragliders and slogans about justified resistance, but it's all in the name of the good cause, right? It's extraordinary how tenacious those old Soviet antisemitic conspiracy theories still are. "Realizing how many American doctors and nurses are Zionists and genuinely terrified for Palestinian, Arab, Muslim, South Asian and Black patients – even more than usual. And usually it's bad," self-described anti-racism campaigner Saira Rao tweeted on January 1, 2024. (Happy new year, Zionist doctors and nurses!) This was just one of many tweets about "Zionist doctors" that went viral in the northern hemisphere winter of 2023–24. These "anti-racist" activists were parroting the Stalinist conspiracy known as the Doctors' Plot, of the early 1950s, when it was rumoured in Moscow that Jewish doctors were scheming to kill Communist Party officials. Hundreds of doctors were arrested, tortured and killed, and many more would have died and been deported had Stalin not died in 1953. Three years later, Nikita Khrushchev admitted it had all been "fabricated ... set up by Stalin", and that it was part of his plan to begin mass deportations of Jews from the Soviet Union.

Would it bother these "progressive" activists to learn they have the same mindset as one of the most psychopathic dictators of all time? Probably not. After all, the hard left has a long tradition of supporting murderous leaders and groups – from Stalin to the Ayatollah Khomeini to even the Houthis – if it's ultimately for the noble cause of standing against capitalism. This is why Corbyn once described Hamas and Hezbollah as "friends" in parliament, and why British hard-left journalists were willing to write deranged puff pieces about Hugo Chávez. The left has never been short of useful idiots.

Oh, but it's not about Jews, activists say. It's about Israel, and that's because, they say, Israel is a colonial country. This claim has become enormously popular since October 7, which is surprising, because it takes a person precisely five seconds (I timed it) to google "the history of Israel" and discover that Israel was originally founded in 1200 BCE, and Jews – like Palestinians – have extremely deep roots there. They are indigenous to the land and were there for about 1400 years, until the Romans arrived and killed the Jews or sold them into slavery. You'd think a story like that (indigenous people! slaves! land stolen!) might attract some sympathy from today's progressive left, but oddly, not. Mainly, I think, because they don't know about it, although there's really no excuse for ignorance in the age of the internet, for heaven's sake – we kids of the '90s had only the *Encyclopaedia Britannica* in the library to teach us this kind of stuff. It is a strange quirk of human development that the more easily information is available, the more ignorant people seem to be. But that's what happens when people rely on hashtags rather than history books for their education.

This leads to the next misconception about Israel: that the British enabled the Jews to colonise it and push out the Palestinians. "You can't convince yesterday's coloniser that today's coloniser is wrong", "You can't choose how resisters resist colonisers" and "Only imperialists stand with Israel" are popular placards at the pro-Palestine marches in London. Because of the 1917 Balfour Declaration and the Mandate for Palestine – when the League of Nations handed Palestine to Britain after the fall of the Ottoman Empire in the wake of World War I – many people on the left believe that Britain partitioned the country and created Israel. Several academics and activists, such as Rashid Khalidi, the Edward Said professor of modern Arab studies at Columbia University, have been especially vociferous in describing Israel as a colonialist state and the current war as "a colonial war".

> *The White Paper was a death sentence for Europe's Jews*

"For the past seventy-five years, Zionism as a movement has been in the business of stabilisation: building the state," says Freedland.

But Zionism's opponents have been in the business of narrative, and the battlegrounds have been on university campuses and academic journals. And they have constructed a very powerful narrative: 1917 imperialism with Britain earmarking land at the Palestinians' expense [in the Balfour Declaration], then 1948 and the Nakba, and then fast-forward to now. It's pretty simple and compelling, this idea that a land was stolen by Britain from people of colour and given to white European Jews. The problem is, that story skips over certain important facts and events. For example, every person on the British left knows about 1920 [when the British took over Mandatory Palestine]. But how many know about 1939?

In fact, Britain increasingly turned away from Zionism throughout the 1930s, starting with the Passfield White Paper in 1930, which argued Jewish immigration to Mandatory Palestine should be limited and land sold only to the Arabs. As Nazism spread across Europe in the early and mid-1930s, Jewish immigration increased as Jews desperately sought refuge from what was coming. This sparked the Arab Revolt of 1936–39, when the Arab political parties in Mandatory Palestine demanded that the British stop allowing Jews into the country, and Britain refused. Lord Robert Peel published the Peel Commission report in 1937, in which he stated that it was impossible to accommodate the rights of both Jews and Arabs in the region – "right against right", as he put it. In 1939, Britain did not have the capacity to deal with revolting Arabs while also facing the inevitability of war in Europe. So in May of that year, it offered another White Paper, which capitulated to all of the Arab demands and offered to give the land to them. The paper also said that Jewish immigration should be limited to 75,000 for the next five years – 15,000 a year – and thereafter be at Arab discretion. This was a death sentence for Europe's Jews, as many Jews recognised, and it was at that moment that the Anglo-Zionist entente ended. But the Arabs rejected the White Paper, partly because they didn't want Jews in their state.

As the war bit across Europe, the Jewish Agency – led by David Ben-Gurion – tried to increase the quotas on Jews allowed into Palestine in order to save them from the Nazis. But the British said no, because they worried it would anger the Arabs – and it probably would have. Although whether that would have been worse than condemning two-thirds of Europe's Jews to be murdered in the Holocaust is a point that can now only be discussed hypothetically.

Even after the war, when it was known exactly what the Jews had suffered, the Arabs didn't want any more Jews in the region and Britain's foreign secretary, Ernest Bevin, did not support the establishment of a Jewish homeland. Nonetheless, the British eventually handed the problem over to the United Nations, who in 1947 decided to partition Palestine into an Arab state and a Jewish state, with Jerusalem to be placed under international trusteeship, and the following year Britain's mandate over the region collapsed. There was an armed Arab uprising against the Jews and hostilities erupted, known in Israel as the War of Independence, during which the State of Israel was declared. It was created, therefore, by legal international mandates as well as war. As the historian Simon Sebag Montefiore wrote in *The Atlantic* in October 2023, "The carving of such states out of these mandates was not exceptional [in the first half of the twentieth century], nor was the imperial promise of separate homelands for different ethnicities or sects unique." Syria, Lebanon, Iraq and Jordan were all conceived in this way by France or Britain in that period. "Imperial powers designed most of the countries in the region, except Egypt," Sebag Montefiore wrote. And with the creation of new states came huge waves of immigration and even full-scale wars, such as that over the partition of India in 1947. Far from being some outlier, "Israel–Palestine was typical."

Typical, but still tragic. The 1948 war and ensuing fall-out was an undeniable tragedy: there was appalling violence on both sides as the Arab states invaded to stop the creation of a Jewish state and kill or at least expel all the Jews there. They failed. They also failed to create a Palestinian state, and over 700,000 Palestinians were forced from their homes in the Nakba.

This, too, was typical of the time: in the aftermath of World War II, ethnic Germans and Italians were – at best – booted out of their homes across Europe. It is estimated that between 14 and 18 million people were displaced and 1 million killed with the partition of India and Pakistan in 1947. That was one of the great tragedies of history, and yet no one is campaigning for the rights of those people to return, because it would simply be unfeasible. After 1948, over 900,000 Jews were kicked out of Islamic countries. They also will never get to return. Tragic, all of it. But typical.

Does it ever give leftists pause for thought that they have this myopic hatred of a country that was founded as a refuge for a people who had been expelled from or slaughtered in every other country? Apparently not – or no more than their deluded belief that Israel is "white". The left always focuses on the European Jews who sought refuge in Israel after the Holocaust (those privileged Holocaust survivors, how dare they?!), but more than half of Israel's Jews came from Middle Eastern countries, such as Iran, Iraq, Egypt and Morocco, which kicked them out. They did not "colonise" Israel. They came to the country of their ancestors, with the support of the United Nations, because it was the only option they had left.

> *They came to the country of their ancestors because it was the only option they had left*

And yet today's progressive leftists treat the creation of Israel as uniquely cruel, uniquely artificial, uniquely unjust.

"In the first half of the twentieth century, millions and millions of Europeans were displaced from their homes along ethnic lines and there was forced migration all around the continent," says Dave Rich. "Look at countries today like Hungary, Slovenia, Romania, Germany: these are all also relatively new countries in terms of where their borders are. And yet only Israel is treated as some kind of fake country dreamed up by Victorian imperialists."

I ask him why this is. "It's because they don't want to have to think about Europe's history," he replies.

> Instead, they can focus on the Jews and make TikToks saying the Jews were these homeless people who the Palestinians took in, out of the goodness of their hearts, and the Jews then stole their country. You have to remember, a lot of modern activists don't even remember the Oslo Accords, never mind the Holocaust, so they can invent a completely false narrative that Israel was created by Western powers as a colony. And why shouldn't they? No one they trust is going to tell them any differently.

Just as the creation of Israel is treated as uniquely unjust, so Israel's treatment of the Palestinians is seen as uniquely cruel.

No question, the Palestinians in the West Bank have suffered terribly since 1967, and it has worsened under Netanyahu. They have endured occupation, violence and injustice, and as I write, about 31,000 Palestinians in Gaza have reportedly been killed by Israeli forces since October 7. This is devastating. It's strange, though, that the same people who march and tweet and shout about the oppression of Palestinians don't also do so about the 1–3 million Uyghurs currently held in concentration camps by the Chinese government, or the genocide of the Rohingya people by the Myanmar government. And none of those perpetrators are compared to the Nazis the way the Israelis are, even though the comparison would be far more apt.

When I say this to people on the progressive left, they tell me I'm comparing numbers – which I agree is bleak and tasteless – or, worse, committing the cardinal debating sin of "whataboutism". Maybe. But then, I suspect they're committing a sin too, which is believing that something is only unacceptable when Jews do it.

That particular sin has a long history, but the roots of its application to Israel can be traced back to the middle of the last century – to 1967, to be exact. My great-uncle Alex, a Polish Jew, was living in Paris when World War II started. Initially he joined the Foreign Legion and was decorated for his courage; he then signed up with the Free French under Charles de Gaulle after France fell to Germany. Alex followed de Gaulle to

England and was devoted to the general – until 1967. By then, Alex owned an art gallery close to the Élysée Palace. In the spring months leading up the Six-Day War, relations between Israel and its neighbouring countries Egypt, Jordan and Syria were deteriorating. De Gaulle, now president of France, warned Israel not to strike first. They ignored him and, in a pre-emptive attack, wiped out most of the Egyptian air force. Thanks to that, they won the war.

De Gaulle, by now a grumpy elder statesman anxious about his fading powers, was extremely irritated that his advice had not been heeded. He held a press conference at the palace in which he described the Jews as "an elite people, domineering and sure of themselves ... [with] ardent and conquering ambition". But 1967 was close enough to the Holocaust for most French people to be horrified by this statement. *Le Monde* ran a cartoon showing a skeleton in a concentration camp with a Star of David on his striped pyjamas with the caption "Sûr de Lui-Même et Dominateur?" (Sure of themselves and domineering?)

My great-uncle Alex was even more horrified: the man he thought of as France's great protector turned out to be just another French traitor of the Jews. So he telephoned his friend, Prime Minister Georges Pompidou, and told him he was sending back his Croix de Guerre and Bronze Star. Pompidou pleaded with him to reconsider, but Alex boxed up his medals, addressed them to the prime minister and the president and had his assistant run them down the road to the palace. Alex had long ago learned that people who looked like friends can swiftly turn against the Jews, and he had no patience for them anymore.

> If Israel made one mistake in the whole of its history, it was winning that war. It was almost instant. It went from victim to oppressor. The sentimental imagination of the left knows no bounds. You cannot – THEY cannot – sympathise with anybody who wins. The minute you win, you've morally lost. To morally win, you have to actually lose.

This is a quote by author Howard Jacobson, used in Jonathan Freedland's play *Jews. In Their Own Words*, which I saw at the Royal Court Theatre in October 2022. I had never before heard such a concise explanation of the left's strange, shifting relationship with Jews and Israel. And like Jacobson and my great-uncle Alex, I date this shift to 1967.

On a geopolitical level, everything changed for Israel after it won the Six-Day War, and not just in the expansion of its territory to include the West Bank, the Golan Heights, the Sinai Peninsula and the Gaza Strip. In the Arab countries, there was a rise of

Islamist politics, as the people there turned against their secular governments in anger about the humiliating defeat. Connected to this was the rise of the Palestine Liberation Organization (PLO), which had a profound impact on how Israel was seen abroad, especially by the left in the West.

General American support for Israel stayed relatively steady for the next forty years, but that was not true for the far left. Campaigning journalists with a strong anti-Israel bias, such as John Pilger in the UK, were gaining prominence. Celebrities such as Vanessa Redgrave openly proclaimed their support for the PLO, even after its members committed appalling terrorist acts, including attacking an Israeli school bus in 1970, killing nine children and three adults, and – most notoriously – massacring eleven Israeli Olympians in Munich in 1972. "Revolutionaries of all countries: unite!" became a global battle cry.

"In the 1960s there was a revolutionary spirit surging through the left all over the world, and people connected Palestine with other liberation causes, such as Vietnam and South Africa," says Rich.

> This fit in with the politics of the time abroad, but also the politics of the time in the Middle East, because the secular Arab governments had been completely discredited by their failures in 1967. So you had this new revolutionary

radicalism of the Palestinian cause, alongside all these other causes animating the global left, because this was a new left generation that had no memory of the war, and their anti-fascist struggle was really about anti-colonialism, and they believed Palestine and Israel fit into that frame.

In June 1976, pro-Palestine terrorists hijacked an Air France plane flying from Tel Aviv to Paris, which was then diverted to Libya and Uganda. My father's best friend, Michel Cojot-Goldberg, and his twelve-year-old son, Olivier, were on that plane. Michel's father had been rounded up during the war and sent to Auschwitz by Klaus Barbie, just because he was Jewish, and Michel thought that now he and Olivier would die for the same reason. From grandfather to father to son. Miraculously, they survived, thanks to the Mossad and the Israeli soldiers who saved all but three of the 106 hostages. Only one Israeli soldier died: Yonatan Netanyahu, elder brother of Binyamin, thereby making the younger man the head of the family. In such ways Israeli history shifts on its axis.

> *What was once seen in the West as a fringe position has moved to the mainstream*

Despite the PLO's regular acts of terrorism against Israelis throughout the 1970s, they were celebrated by some in the West as freedom fighters. There was a "radical chic" – to use Tom Wolfe's phrase about white liberals who supported the Black Panthers during this period – in supporting the PLO. But the difference between then and now is that in the 1970s, there weren't massive demonstrations in support of the killers of Israeli athletes, or the hijackers of Air France's plane. But there are demonstrations of support for the October 7 pogrom. What was once seen in the West as a wacky, fringe position has moved to the mainstream.

Just as significantly, Israeli politics shifted during the 1970s and '80s. "The occupation became more set in stone, then in 1977 Israel gets its first right-wing government," says Rich. "More settlements are built, then it's the Lebanon War in 1982, which was the first time the Western media covered an Israeli war the way it covers them now, focusing on the undoubted suffering of the Palestinians, the increasingly right-wing Israeli government and a radicalised Palestinian movement, so a lot of things were coalescing."

Many things can be true: Israel became much more aggressive after 1967, and certainly more powerful. But the PLO was at least as aggressive, if not as powerful. Maybe, as Jacobson says, the left simply preferred underdogs. Or maybe something else was going on. One question I've often asked myself is: why did de Gaulle not want Israel to strike first? Why was he so angry when they won the war? Did he just want to feel some semblance of control over Israel? Or did he – like so many others – have a subconscious preference to keep Jews in a supine position, and felt a fear that slipped into anger when they refused to remain submissive and obedient?

After October 7, many politicians on the left, especially in the UK and US, felt compelled to share their thoughts about how Israel should react to the vicious pogrom. Like de Gaulle, they thought Israel should do nothing. It is very hard to imagine 150 British Labour councillors feeling entitled to lecture, say, Australia, about how to conduct itself just after had it been brutally attacked. Just two weeks after October 7, an associate professor of Holocaust and genocide studies argued in *The Guardian* that Israel must stop "weaponising" the Holocaust, but that October 7 should be seen within "the historical context of Israeli settler colonialism". So Israel shouldn't mention the Holocaust – in which two-thirds of Europe's Jews were wiped out – when discussing Hamas, whose original charter called for a genocide of the Jews (which you'd think a professor of genocide might mention in his article, but no). But the 1948 Arab–Israeli War should be cited – weaponised, even – in discussions of the recent pogrom. Got it. This paradox is common parlance on the left after October 7: the Holocaust is irrelevant, the 1948 war essential. The mental contortions some people will adopt to justify violence against Israel, and to argue that Israel has no right to defend itself, really are extraordinary.

Some will argue that the death toll in Gaza since October proves that these intellectual descendants of de Gaulle were right: Israel shouldn't have retaliated. But I find this mentality baffling. The scale of civilian deaths in this war is horrific, and Israel should be doing more to minimise them and to allow more aid to reach the Palestinians. But Hamas put Israel into an impossible position, having to defeat an enemy that deliberately embeds itself in hospitals and other heavily populated areas, an enemy that has specifically said it wants to wipe Israel off the map. What other country would be chided by outsiders after 1200 of its citizens had been so brutally murdered and 250 taken hostage? When the killers crowed about their savagery and promised to do it again? Why is Israel so entirely blamed for attacking Hamas, and Hamas given a free pass for using their own citizens as human shields? Why do people on the left not care when Muslims kill Muslims, or – in the context of Israel and Palestine – Muslims kill Jews, but Jews killing Muslims drives them completely insane with rage? What is it about Israel that attracts such a disproportionate amount of attention from the West? I used to think that maybe Westerners hold Israel to a higher standard and that their so-called support for Palestinians is actually just the racism of low expectations.

After all, Palestinians deserve better than Hamas and it's strange that more activists don't say this.

Progressive activists insist Israel must find "a peaceful solution", which is clearly an impossible command given that Hamas is determined to eradicate it. And I increasingly feel like the impossibility is deliberate. Antisemites mock Jews for going meekly to the concentration camps like lambs; but when Jews fight back, our alleged allies tell us we're too elite, domineering and sure of ourselves.

With Gaza so destroyed now, and the Palestinians suffering so much in the West Bank, it is impossible not to think back with some bitterness to the Camp David summit in 2000, when US president Bill Clinton and Israeli prime minister Ehud Barak offered PLO leader Yasser Arafat the greatest concessions ever offered by Israel, and Arafat said no. Furious and frustrated, Clinton banged the table with his fist and said, "You are leading your people and the region to a catastrophe." An accurate prediction on his part. The Palestinian leadership had no interest in compromise; only the river to the sea was enough – sometimes because that's what they really

> *The story of Israel and Palestine is far more complex, interesting and tragic than the simplistic one painted by Western activists*

believed, sometimes because it was in their interest to keep the conflict going. Netanyahu has been no better. Over the past two decades he has repeatedly rejected opportunities to engage with the Palestinians, and his political career pretty much depends on sustaining the current conflict. So it's impossible not to think back, with even more bitterness, to the assassination of Yitzhak Rabin in 1995, killed by a far-right Israeli furious with Rabin for having signed the Oslo Accords.

The story of Israel and Palestine is far more complex, interesting and tragic than the simplistic one painted by Western activists today. It is one of missed opportunities, exploitative politicians and exploited people. It is entirely reasonable to sympathise with the Palestinians' sense of aggrievement at losing their land in 1948, and even their resentment at having to share it – but not to the point of condoning Palestinian terrorism against Israelis.

In December 2023, South Africa accused Israel of committing genocide against the Palestinians, and surrealist absurdity peaked. A genocide is an intention "to destroy, in whole or in part, a national, ethnical, racial or religious group", and the only people in this war determined to wipe out a nation are Hamas. Israel caused enormous casualties, and certainly members of Netanyahu's cabinet have made horrifically homicidal threats against the Palestinians. But Israel's initial action was self-defence, proven by the fact they were attacked first, something

South Africa seems to have missed. By accusing Israel of genocide, South Africa showed the efficacy of Hamas's strategy of embedding itself among its own people, thereby designing a war that guarantees the deaths of its own citizens.

South Africa's credulous and self-serving accusation was a magnificent PR victory for Hamas, which only months earlier had filmed itself murdering Israelis. Ultimately, the International Court of Justice prevaricated and took the middle road, saying Israel must ensure it doesn't commit genocide, and reminded Hamas that it, too, was bound by humanitarian law and it should release the hostages. That second part of the ruling was ignored by the far-left activists in the US and UK, who crowed on social media that Israel had been condemned for genocide. It had not.

If South Africa had accused Israel of war crimes in regard to Netanyahu's cruel withholding of humanitarian essentials for people in Gaza, then it would have had a case. But accusing Israel of genocide – as opposed to the actually and openly genocidal Hamas – proved that something else was going on. Like the desire to de-Jew Holocaust Memorial Day, accusing Israelis and Jews of genocide – of being "worse than Nazis", as the frequent insult has it – means any guilt about the Holocaust can melt away. The Jews have done it too, so World War II is cancelled out – that's the thinking, I guess. The far left – in ways very similar to the far right – has never wanted to accept that Jews have, throughout history, been terrorised, because to accept that means they cannot hate them. And so they erase Jewish history by rewriting the Holocaust and insisting that the war in Gaza is literally the same as Auschwitz, when one is a bitter war of retribution and the other was a specifically designed death camp. One has resulted in – so far – 31,000 Palestinian deaths, according to Hamas figures, including a contested number of militants. The other was the industrial annihilation of 6 million Jews. The Jewish population is only just starting to reach pre-1939 levels again, having taken eighty years to recover from Hitler's genocide. The Palestinian population, on the other hand, will continue to grow, and as Sebag Montefiore writes, demographic numbers are a good indicator of where genocide has actually been committed. But that's irrelevant for the progressive left, which only cares about preserving its precious value system, which by now is predicated on a crucial rule: the Jew is never the victim. So the Jew can always be hated.

The progressive left

A sentence I never imagined I'd write: I now think Jeremy Corbyn did Jews in Britain a favour. Corbyn was the leader of the Labour Party in the UK from 2015 to 2020 and the most far-left leader of the party for decades. The Equalities and Human Rights

Commission (EHRC) had other descriptions for him when it investigated Labour in 2020 and found that, under Corbyn, the party was guilty of harassing and discriminating against Jews. Labour, the EHRC decreed, had broken the law. Corbyn and his very vocal acolytes reacted as they'd done for the past five years whenever Jews within the party raised concerns: they insisted it was all malicious lies to undermine a good socialist.

The Corbyn era was an extremely weird time for British Jews, but an eye-opening one, and I now think it prepared many of us for the left's reaction to October 7, whereas American Jews I know seemed far more surprised. The gaslighting (it didn't happen), the defences (and if it did, they deserved it), the hectoring moral superiority

> *The left doesn't care about antisemitism if they deem it inconvenient to their cause*

(how can you care about *that* when *this* is so much more important?): all that we saw after October 7, we had seen under Corbyn. It also woke me up to something that I really hadn't understood before: the progressive left hates the Jews.

Now is not the place to rehash the (many) examples of Corbyn's jaw-dropping attitudes towards Jews, never mind Israel, ideas some of us naively thought had died out with Stalin. Those are specific to Corbyn, whose political relevance is now, thankfully, in the past. But two general truths emerged from that era that would prove extremely relevant after October 7. The first was how little people across the left cared when Jews pointed out the obvious antisemitism they saw in the Labour Party. In 2018, 86 per cent of British Jews said they believed Corbyn was antisemitic, and still the left supported him, and still *The Guardian* backed him in the 2019 general election. Would they – good lefties one and all, bulwarks against oppression – have done this if the vast majority of another minority said they believed Corbyn was bigoted against them? Would the left have supported an Islamophobic leader in 2018? A homophobic one? A racist one? It's hard to imagine. "What are Jews so scared of? It's not like Corbyn's going to bring back pogroms," a prominent figure on the left asked me. I briefly amused myself by imagining a response: "Why are Black people so against the Tories? It's not like they'll bring back lynching." But I stayed schtum.

The left doesn't care about antisemitism if they deem it inconvenient to their cause. They just call it "anti-Zionism" and carry on, and that was – it turned out – a good lesson to learn. There was another lesson, too. Corbyn railed frequently against the horrors of Israel, and yet he had frequently been a paid contributor to Iranian and Russian state TV. He had referred to Hamas and Hezbollah as "friends" in a parliamentary meeting, and after October 7 initially refused to describe Hamas as a terrorist group. None of this dented his extraordinary popularity with the progressive left. I expected little better of the older members of the far left – the grizzled old guys who had been going to Socialist Workers Party events since the early '80s, like Corbyn himself. But I was surprised by how little Corbyn's hypocrisy and blindness to Islamist terrorism bothered the young progressive left. Then he was pushed out of Labour in 2020 and I dismissed him as a classic useful idiot – which was right – and a blip, an aberration, one I needn't think about again – which was wrong. Because then October 7 happened. I realised that the Corbyn era had opened a Pandora's box and some ghosts cannot be controlled.

Antisemitism found a new point of entry through identity politics, which was developed on US and – to a lesser degree – UK university campuses over the past twenty years. This ideology has now escaped to the wider world as students schooled in it have moved into workplaces. Identity politics argues that in order to see the world clearly, we need to divide it up into particular group identities, specifically racial and sexual identities, and quantify the degrees of their oppression. As Yascha Mounk writes in *The Identity Trap*, adherents of identity politics believe that, in the name of fairness, liberal democracies need to jettison universal values such as free speech and respect for diverse opinions – values long championed by the Jewish Diaspora. Instead, we should now see everyone through the prisms of race and sexual orientation and treat them differently, depending on their identity group and how much oppression they have historically suffered. With its rules, rigidity and belief that academic theories must be applied universally in the real world, identity politics is profoundly illiberal and a sharp contrast to the kind of liberalism that defined the mainstream left in the West for the past eighty or so years.

In order to make this simplistic ideology even more simple, identity politics divides the world into two racial categories: "white" (defined as colonising oppressors) and "people of colour" (the oppressed). This is how the left pivoted from talking about class to talking about race. It is also why antisemitism is thriving again on campuses, as supporters of identity politics combine with activists for Black and Muslim causes, who see Jews as ultra white and therefore oppressive. And, to be clear, those activists aren't necessarily Black or Muslim themselves; in fact, as multiple students have told me, these activists are often white, but see supporting these causes – and trashing Israel and Jews – as a means of proving their allyship and exonerating themselves from white guilt.

Identity politics has proven astonishingly influential, especially in shaping US and UK policies, and no doubt many people pushing it are motivated by good intentions. (Some, of course, are pure grifters.) I initially assumed that a fear of being called racist had lobotomised them so they were unable to see the obvious idiocies of this ideology. (Is a poor white man in Glamorgan really more privileged than an extremely wealthy Black man in Nairobi?) But the more identity politics took hold, the more I understood that a lot of people on the left just want a very simple way of looking at the world, and they crave a group they can hate with impunity.

One of the biggest problems with identity politics is its inability to accommodate competing rights, and the idea that two groups can both be right. ("Right against right," as Lord Peel put it.) I got a glimpse of this in 2015, when I started to write about gender ideology, which argues that trans women should be accorded all the rights biological women have, such as access to female single-sex spaces. The problems seemed glaring to me, but as I quickly learned, asking any questions at all about the conflict of rights between those of women and trans women sparked furious accusations of transphobia from the progressive left.

> *Because of the left-wing antisemitic stereotypes about them, Jews aren't just white, they are ultra-white*

Identity politics is a zero-sum game, and for one group to be all good, the group with competing rights must be all bad. So, in the case of gender ideology, trans people are all good ("trans people are sacred", as the popular hashtag on social media has it), and women who are anxious about the erosion of their rights are evil. I strongly believe that the most vicious abuse I get for my defence of women's rights is actually about misogyny, but identity politics gave left-wing men a self-righteous cover so they could deride women like me, and feel morally superior for doing so.

It's a similar story with the progressive left's reaction to Israel and Palestine: a lot of it is about antisemitism, but identity politics obscures the bigotry, giving the left a preeningly self-righteous excuse to ignore Hamas's terrorism and violence against Jews. This comparison between how women and Jews are discussed in identity politics is not original to me. In February 2024 Corinne Blacker wrote in *Tablet* magazine that, thanks to the energetic efforts of gender ideologue and anti-Israel academic Judith Butler, antisemitism has been "queered", meaning anyone who supports Israel's right to exist is seen as analogous to a bigot who hates trans people. Only trans people and Palestinians are seen as oppressed, and never women or Jews.

In March 2024, the progressive literary magazine *Guernica* took down an article by Joanna Chen, an Israeli translator who works for a non-profit that helps Palestinians, because it dared to express sorrow for the Israeli hostages as well as the people in Gaza. This, *Guernica*'s publisher explained, made the article "an apologia for Zionism and the ongoing genocide in Gaza".

In fact, Chen's article was the opposite. But it didn't paint Israelis as uniformly evil, and so it had to be deleted.

"For all the very clever people who exist in progressive discourse, they do very badly want morally, emotionally and psychologically to feel that they are on the right side of history," says Baddiel. "By that, they mean supporting the vulnerable against the forces of power, and Jews are the only minority – certainly in the West – who are associated with power."

Jews Don't Count was published two years before October 7 and it addresses why the left is so antipathetic to the idea of Jews being oppressed. Baddiel memorably describes Jews as "Schrödinger's whites", meaning their whiteness depends on the politics of the observer. The far right sees them as suspicious, foreign and not white, whereas the left sees them as extremely white because they can pass as non-Jews. In fact, because of the left-wing antisemitic stereotypes about them – that they're rich and powerful oppressors – they aren't just white, they are ultra-white.

Since October 7, this perception of Jews and Israelis as being extra-white has been especially popular. "YOU'RE EITHER ON THE WHITE OR RIGHT SIDE OF HISTORY", one popular march placard has it, with images of the Israeli, British, American and French flags on one side, and the flags for Palestine, East Turkestan, the DRC and Sudan on the other. Never mind that around half of Israelis are Mizrahi, meaning they have roots in North Africa and all over the Middle East, and are descended from the Jews who were kicked out of those regions in 1948. So, very much not white.

While I was working on this article, it emerged that a BBC controller had been posting antisemitic screeds on Facebook, referring to Jews as "a bunch of subcontinental European recessive CaucAsian japhetic AskeNazis who have None zero zilch blood connection to the land of Palestine or Israel historically" and "a subcontinental Caucasian invader coloniser species with zero indigenous blood". (She was suspended after a US publication exposed this, but it's hard to believe no one at the BBC had previously noticed her posts or beliefs.)

Another of the central tenets of identity politics is that all oppressions are linked, so LGBTQ+ rights are the same as Palestinian rights, and so on (never mind that same-sex sexual activity is illegal in Gaza). Consider the sign outside an independent bookshop not far from my house that promises books about:

Palestine
Feminist
LGBTQ+
Black Struggle
Migrants

This is why so many Western activists – especially in the US – see the Palestinians as akin to black slaves and the Israelis as plantation owners, with a total lack of embarrassment about their historical ignorance. But the progressive left's determination to see the Middle East through the prism of the US and UK reveals their arrogance and their ignorance. And given how horrified they profess to be about colonialism, it is a ludicrous irony that they narcissistically colonise the Middle East conflict with their own – entirely different, entirely irrelevant – Western issues. Israel and Palestine have nothing in common with the gay rights movement in the US or the desegregation of the American South, and while stupidity plays a big part in why so many people in the West believe otherwise, there are other issues, too.

"Jews have always been a glitch in the binary of identity politics"

For some people online with big followings, there's a lot of brand-building going on here, as they loudly reassure their followers that Palestine and Israel are a simple matter of good versus evil. Few things attract more followers on social media than someone reassuring them that they're good and this other group is bad.

But the enthusiasm with which the West has taken up this idea suggests something else, too: how better to absolve your guilt about your own country's historical wrongs than by dumping them on other countries now? The sheer volume of comparisons between anti-Black racism and Israel and Palestine coming especially from American activists strongly hints that there is more than a little displacement going on, and identity politics enables it. It is, I think, no coincidence that it was South Africa that accused Israel of genocide. South Africa has been calling Israel an "apartheid state" for years, but any suggestion that it should be seen as the conscience of the world, as some high-profile progressives have said in the past few months, is laughable. For a start, South Africa is one of a very select group of countries that has diplomatic relations with Hamas, and so was predictably slow to speak up about October 7. It was even slower to speak out against Russia's invasion of Ukraine. In a final twist of gruesome irony, only a week before South Africa accused Israel of genocide, the country's president, Cyril Ramaphosa, welcomed Mohamed Hamdan Dagalo, a Sudanese warlord whose militia is accused of genocide in Darfur. Still, what better way to cleanse oneself of uncomfortable accusations than to point the finger at someone else?

"This idea that Israel is a racist country, that has been around since the '60s and was part of Soviet and PLO propaganda, and the UN motion in 1975," Rich says, referring to the United Nations General Assembly Resolution 3379, which determined that Zionism was a form of racism and racial discrimination. It was sponsored by the Arab League and several African countries. The US and UK both voted against it, but the resolution passed with seventy-two votes (thirty-two abstentions, thirty-five against). The great American diplomat Daniel Patrick Moynihan warned before the vote, "The United Nations is about to make antisemitism international law … a great evil has been loosed upon the world." In 1991 the UN General Assembly revoked the resolution. "But that idea *really* resonates now because it absolutely fits with the zeitgeist of what progressive left politics is all about, which is race. So all the pieces were there, but they suddenly clicked," says Rich.

Identity politics simplifies the world into literal black and white. But Jews complicate this because they are historically oppressed and yet are seen as successful and, in regards to Israel, in a position of power over the Palestinians. "Jews have always been a glitch in the binary of identity politics, and Israel is a glitch in it, because colonisation as an idea is completely wrong, but at the same time, most colonisers were not refugees," says Baddiel.

> But if you see the world this way, only in terms of the victimisers of the victimised, then you don't see Jews as the victimised because they're seen as white. So when Jews talk about antisemitism, I think it sounds to a lot

of people like posh aristocrats claiming there's a leak in their ancestral home when everyone else is going through a cost-of-living crisis.

Is it a resentment that Jews have this trump card of oppression – Holocaust! We win! – that makes people deny the history? Or are they so blinded by their own prejudices that they mentally filter out any facts that contradict their narrative? In November 2023, the actress Susan Sarandon spoke at a pro-Palestine rally in New York, declaring that Jews who were feeling fearful of the rising antisemitism were "getting a taste of what it feels like to be Muslim in this country, so often subjected to violence".

She was then dropped by her talent agency and apologised on social media, saying "the phrasing was a terrible mistake". But there's no possible phrasing that would have made it better, because the sentiment was plain. Sarandon was clearly so wedded to the idea of Palestinians as victims and Jews as privileged oppressors that she could block out the murder of eleven Jews in Pittsburgh's Tree of Life synagogue in 2018, the murder of four people in a targeted attack on a kosher deli in Jersey City the following year, the attack on a Texas synagogue in 2022 during which four Jews were taken hostage by a gunman, and so on. Jews are, in fact, the biggest target of religious hate crimes in the US by an enormous margin. And that's not even counting that – in living memory – American universities used to have quotas on the number of Jews admitted, and that Jews were explicitly or implicitly excluded from many sections of American public life well into the mid-twentieth century. I don't know why actors are invited to talk about anything, given their literal job is to speak words other people have written for them. But Sarandon gave a handy insight into the amorality – or simple stupidity – required to subscribe to this progressive-left antisemitism.

It's been an especially strange time to be a Jewish woman on the left. When we explain why we might not want trans women in our single-sex spaces, referring to past experiences of male violence, we are accused of "weaponising our trauma". When we talk about our fear of Hamas, because Jews have some experience when it comes to genocidal fascist groups, we're accused of "weaponising the Holocaust". Women in general – like Jews – tend not to be believed anyway when they describe violence committed against them. After all, according to a recent annual report from the victims' commissioner for England and Wales, only 5 per cent of reported rapes result in charges being brought, never mind convictions. So when stories started to emerge fairly soon after October 7

> *It took UN Women fifty days even to acknowledge that these sexual assaults had happened*

that Hamas had committed horrific sexual violence during the pogrom, I knew the reaction would be bad. I hoped, given we'd so recently come through the #MeToo movement, with its urgent messaging that women should be believed, that it wouldn't be too bad. I was wrong.

The October 7 rapes of Israeli women – and men – were so brutal that Meni Binyamin, the head of the International Crime Investigations Unit of the Israeli police, said it was "the most extreme sexual abuses we have seen". One woman was found with a knife in her vagina and her internal organs removed. Others were shot in the vagina and breasts. Witnesses reported a woman begging to be killed as she was passed between Hamas fighters, a woman being stabbed in the back while she was raped, terrorists cutting off a woman's breast and playing with it in the road.

It took UN Women fifty days even to acknowledge that these sexual assaults had happened. When Reem Alsalem, the UN special rapporteur on violence against women and girls, was asked why, she reportedly replied that the evidence of rape was "not solid", even though there was video footage of Israeli women with blood-sodden crotches and reports from witnesses about dead Israeli women's mutilated vaginas. On October 30, almost 150 "scholars in feminist, queer and trans studies" signed an open letter implying that to support Israeli women was to endorse "colonial feminism". Not a single UK charity that purports to protect women from violence condemned Hamas's brutality – except Jewish Women's Aid. Southall Black Sisters expressed sympathy for people killed in Gaza and Israel, but entirely overlooked Hamas's taking of hostages when calling out contraventions of international law. Sisters Uncut, which was formed in reaction to the UK's government's cuts to services for victims of domestic violence, staged a sit-in at Liverpool Street Station demanding an Israeli ceasefire. After I wrote an article in the *Jewish Chronicle* asking how this fitted in with their feminist credentials, they replied with a statement saying that the reports of Israeli women being raped were merely "the Islamophobic and racist weaponisation of sexual violence that presents it as an Arab, as opposed to a global, problem".

In an attempt to make people believe what had actually happened on October 7, the IDF compiled and edited the footage they had from Hamas's GoPro cameras, made it into a film, called *Bearing Witness*, and took it around the world to show small, carefully selected audiences. Most journalists who watched it wrote afterwards about how traumatising they found it. Others had different reactions.

The far-left activist Owen Jones, *The Guardian*'s most highprofile journalist, went to a screening of *Bearing Witness* and afterwards posted a twenty-five-minute video review. He claimed that "the purpose of the film was made very clear: that we were to 'bear witness', as it was repeatedly put, to the horrors committed by Hamas and also make the PR case for Israel's onslaught against Gaza". Others who attended the screening told me that no one said any such thing – the purpose was to provide video footage of the pogrom. Jones said, "If there was rape and sexual violence committed, we don't see that on camera," apparently unaware that the IDF had already said it only included footage that "preserved the dignity" of those killed. The body of a burnt woman with no underwear on "is not what you consider conclusive evidence of rape", he said. And while he was raising a sceptical eyebrow over the bodies of dead, naked Israeli women, he parroted unquestioningly figures from Hamas about the number of Palestinian civilians killed in the war.

Jones epitomises the modern far left. He initially made a name writing about social class. By the mid-2010s, he was focusing increasingly on identity politics, especially trans issues, and he devotes an extraordinary amount of time to describing women who have concerns about gender ideology as bigots. Now, he tweets primarily about Palestine and calls anyone who disagrees with him a defender of genocide. So this global shrugging at or scepticism about the rapes of Israeli women was the perfect crescendo to this move in the progressive left of, first, dismissing women and, next, dismissing Jews. "Ultimately, all this is about politics here, not about politics in Israel," says Rich.

Clearly Hamas is extremely far from the left. But the interesting thing about identity politics is that you have your identity, and everything blindly flows from that. You cannot underestimate how unthinking so much of this. People on the progressive left just think, "Right, Palestine is our side, so of course we hate Israel." So much of it is just performative.

Performative and toxic. And when progressive-left identity politics takes you to a place where you are jazz hands-ing away the rapes of Israeli women by fascist Islamists, maybe you should ask yourself if this movement has outlived its purpose.

Identity politics has filled the gap left by the fall of communism, when people on the left could identify as part of a distinct tribe and duly subscribe to all of its beliefs, no matter how absurd, self-defeating and cruel. It is the "set menu" approach to politics, as Lionel Shriver put it in October 2023, when you think of yourself as being on the far left and so obediently support everyone ostensibly in that camp, even if it's just because they're the opponents to your chosen enemy, as is the case with Hamas. It reveals such vanity, but also such bankrupt intelligence, this desire to outsource any critical thinking to an external, prefabricated ideology. And identity politics, like communism, like fascism, gives licence to its followers to celebrate sadism and dehumanise entire demographics. Perhaps the thing that surprises me the most about human nature, even in my mature middle age, is how enduring this desire is.

The future

So what next? That's what Jews ask one another when they meet. It's what I asked everyone I spoke to for this essay. What happens next? How fearful should we be? Should we keep the suitcase by the door? And where would we go?

While researching this essay, one common concern was expressed repeatedly by British Jews I interviewed: the failure of state institutions to protect them. "It has been an enormous shock to see the great institutions of state turn on the Jews," Anthony Julius told me, citing the universities for failing to quash antisemitism on campus, the police for not stopping calls for jihad and Jewish genocide on the pro-Palestine marches, and the BBC for, in particular, its initial blithe speculation that Israel had bombed the al-Ahli hospital in Gaza City, which turned out to be false. In February, an employment tribunal ruled that "anti-Zionist beliefs qualified … as a protected characteristic", in a case that found that the virulently antisemitic professor of sociology David Miller had been unfairly sacked by Bristol University.

Miller has publicly said that "to dismantle the regime, every single Zionist organisation, the world over, needs to be ended. Every. Single. One", and that Jewish students who join the university's Jewish societies are "assets of Israel". As British-Jewish academic David Hirsh wrote after the verdict, "By determining that anti-Zionism is protected, but without considering the issue of antisemitism, the tribunal risks protecting antisemites against Jews. It risks turning the *Equality Act* on its head, making its effect the very opposite of what was intended." The night after the ruling came in, I happened to go to a book launch by a British-Jewish author, and every single conversation I had with other Jews was about this effective legalisation of antisemitism. The feeling of shock in the room was palpable.

> *Why read up on the history of the Levant when you can just scroll through TikTok and Instagram instead?*

Of less surprise has been the response of the UN, which was characteristically slow to condemn the October 7 pogrom. The revelation that some United Nations Relief and Works Agency (UNRWA) staff were Hamas members, and even participated in the terrorism, did not surprise many longstanding observers of the agency. When a network of Hamas tunnels was discovered beneath the UNRWA headquarters in Gaza in February

2024, certain members of the far left dismissed it as propaganda. "Israel lies and lies and lies again," said Owen Jones.

My biggest worry – as I started this essay and still as I end it – is the younger generation. Every study shows that the younger a person is in the West, the more anti-Israel they are. This is likely a reflection that most young people associate Israel with Netanyahu, who has been the country's prime minister for most of their lives. (Although why they don't have similar negative feelings about Palestine, given that Hamas has been in charge there in Gaza for a similar length of time, is a separate question.) Alongside that, one in five young Americans (aged eighteen to twenty-nine) believe that the Holocaust is a myth, and a study conducted by the ADL in December 2023 found there is a heavy overlap between anti-Israel sentiments and anti-Jewish ones (no surprise there to anyone with eyes, ears and a brain). This same study found that 85 per cent of Americans across the age groups believe in at least one antisemitic trope – such as that American Jews are more loyal to Israel than to America, or that Jews have too much power in the business world – a huge increase from 61 per cent only four years earlier.

Once I'd have thought that the radical chic of the young would dim the more they learned about the history of the Middle East, but that no longer feels like a given. We are living in an age of almost wilful ignorance and blinkered partisanship.

News organisations in the US and UK are largely very politically partisan, but at least they are (mostly) forced to adhere to some standards of accuracy. Yet most young people don't even bother reading a newspaper or watching the news. They rely on extremely questionable online sources and, of course, social media to tell them what's happening and what to think about it. Most people have the world's knowledge in their pockets thanks to their smartphones, but those same devices have destroyed people's attention spans – and why read up on the history of the Levant when you can just scroll through TikTok and Instagram instead? They have also given rise to an age of conspiracy theories – whether about vaccinations or the US election – and this is a testament to this general deterioration of critical thinking and overexposure to the internet. More than any other age group, teenagers are most likely to believe conspiracy theories, and antisemitism is, above all else, a conspiracy theory – the original one, even. To believers, it explains why their lives aren't as they wish, because Jews, that malevolent shadowy cabal, are hoarding all the power and money.

The images of desperate, wounded and dead Palestinians are only compounding the anti-Israel and antisemitic leanings of the younger generation. The news has become, for most people, unwatchably sad. But after spending two months working on this piece, I end it feeling as confused as when I began: why is it impossible for so many on the left to feel enormous compassion for the Palestinians and also to understand that Israel cannot live alongside a terrorist group dedicated to its extermination? When I say this, some people accuse me of being pro-war, which I'm not. I dearly wish Israel hadn't killed so many Palestinians since October 7. Netanyahu walked directly into the trap laid by Hamas, as so many of us feared he would. The left sees Netanyahu's actions, but they refuse to see the manoeuvrings of Hamas, baiting Israel with the savage pogrom and then sacrificing their own people during Israel's entirely foreseeable unrelenting retaliation. Why are they only angry at Israel for fighting back, and not also at Hamas for failing to protect its people – by committing October 7, by still retaining hostages, by totally failing to take any measures to shelter the people they purportedly represent? What is the point in calling for a ceasefire when Hamas refuses to accept Israel's right to exist? I can chalk it up to antisemitism, and I largely do. But it still feels astonishing to me, so many people around the world forsaking honest clarity and critical thought for easy partisanship.

But one thing has changed during the course of writing this: I feel a little more optimistic. Back in December 2023, I felt almost desperate with anxiety, certain the West was about to turn against the Jews, again. I don't think that so much anymore. The brutality of Israel's onslaught against Hamas is shocking to see, but I know that a lot of people have also been taken aback by the far left's antagonism to Israel – and to Jews – after October 7. The "river to the sea" chanters might have the louder voices, but I suspect they are outnumbered by the quiet moderates who have been astonished by the eagerness of so-called progressives to justify violence against Israelis. Israel pummelling Gaza City into dust was, sadly, not a surprise, but vocal feminists suddenly describing rapes as mere "resistance" was a big surprise to many. So many non-Jews over the past few months have approached me to voice their disquiet about the vicious anti-Israeli views of their colleague, their friend, their once favourite newspaper columnist. Anecdotally, I hear of increasing numbers of London schools contacting high-profile Jews to come in and talk to the students and try to introduce some shades of grey to the teenagers' furiously black-and-white beliefs about Israel and Palestine.

> *In the absence of guarantees about the future, isn't it better to keep the dream alive in the present?*

President Biden and major European leaders have continued to affirm Israel's right to defend itself, while increasingly adding qualifiers that more care needs to be taken about minimising civilian casualties and providing humanitarian aid to the Palestinians. But they are not defending Hamas or calling October 7 "resistance". And at this point, clearing even that low bar feels like a mercy. "In the 1920s and '30s, governments across Europe turned against the Jewish community, and that is absolutely not what's happening now," says Rich. "I know many Jews feel scared of the size of the [pro-Palestine] protests, but … these people do not have any sort of purchase in where power actually resides, so it all goes on the street." Speaking as one who went on many anti-Brexit and anti-Trump marches between 2016 and 2020, I can confirm Rich's point about their lack of impact.

But there is a reason Jews are feeling the antisemitism so deeply this time round. "It is predominantly in parts of society where a lot of Jews are living and working," Rich explains. "So you see it in liberal, diverse professions, in the media and arts sectors. The kind of antisemitism you get in working-class industries and small towns – it's there, but it's not this type, and it's not as toxic. Now it's affecting the communities where Jews live." And that is horrible, as I know. But it would be a lot more horrible if the US president was tearing down posters of kidnapped Israeli children rather than an artist in my neighbourhood. That may happen one day – after all, the twenty-somethings on today's marches chanting "From the river to the sea" will one day sit in the seats of power, and there is no reason to believe they'll have changed their thinking by then. But for now, they're not.

A two-state solution for Israel and Palestine has rarely felt so distant. And yet, it may be that this horrific conflict ultimately leads to it, if the Israelis and Palestinians – never mind their current dreadful leadership – ultimately come together to achieve it, exhausted by all the pain caused by life without it. That will sound stupidly kumbaya optimistic to some. But in the absence of guarantees about the future, isn't it better to keep the dream alive in the present, to not be changed and curdled by anxiety, hate and revenge? Because we have surely now reached – oh God, please – rock bottom here. Surely.

This morning I walked my children to school, past the bridge, as always. As usual, the ground was covered in the most miserable kind of confetti, the remnants of ripped-up hostage posters. A woman was standing with her back to me, and I instinctively reached for my kids, thinking she had torn down the posters. But as I got closer, I saw it was a different person, and she had a clutch of papers under her arm. They were hostage posters, and she was posting them up on the sidings of the bridge. As she heard us approach, she turned around quickly, presumably used to being shouted at for doing this. We looked in each other's eyes for a beat, nodded, smiled, and then we both carried on. ≡

www.ingramcontent.com/pod-product-compliance
Lightning Source LLC
Chambersburg PA
CBHW030122170426
43198CB00009B/712